POSITIVE
SELF-TALK

SHANI T. NIGHT

 INFINITE GENERATIONS PUBLISHING

Intentionally Positive

Live to inspire the next generation.

- Shani T. Night

Paperback ISBN: 978-1-953364-50-0

Copyright © 2024 Shani T. Night.

Infinite Generations
137 National Plaza, STE 300
National Harbor, MD 20745

Printed in the United States of America

First Printing, 2024

Art by Canva
Cover Design by: I Howard and D. Spruill

POSITIVE MEDIA, HAPPY LIFE

WWW.INFINITEGENERATIONS.COM

I dedicate this book to the restless souls, to those in search of more, and to those acknowledging an innate awareness that there's a greater depth to explore. To those ready to empower themselves, recognizing the immense strength within their inner voice. I extend these words to you as a guide to the essence of joy. Within these pages, I share the wisdom that resonates deeply within my soul, for it is my earnest belief that your journey toward happiness commences with self-awareness and self-care. May you embrace this moment and the unfolding days, prioritizing what truly matters to cultivate a life of profound fulfillment and joy. Your well-being begins with you, and as you embark on this transformative exploration, may it lead you to the abundant joy that resides within your own heart.

Dear Reader:

Thank you for your purchase.
I hope you enjoy Positive Self-Talk.

Please share a review of this book on Amazon.

Visit my website for more content, discounts, contests, giveaways,
and/or a free consult.
www.shanitnight.com

 Follow Shani Night:
instagram.com/shaninight
www.facebook.com/ShaniTNight
I post daily/weekly positive messages.

"I ASPIRE TO BE THE
BEST PART OF ME."

SHANI T. NIGHT

POSITIVE THOUGHT

POSITIVE RESULT

Dive into the transformative journey of 'Positive Self-Talk,' an empowering guide that unveils 20 essential insights into the world of positive self-dialogue.

Uncover the roots of negative self-talk as you navigate through a guide designed to encourage reflection and promote a fresh and positive mindset. That's not all – this book is your toolkit with 21 dynamic exercises meticulously designed to build and strengthen your positive self-talk muscle.

From understanding the origins of negativity to mastering the art of self-affirmation, embark on a path of self-discovery and empowerment. 'Positive Self-Talk' is not just a book; it's your companion in the quest for a more confident, resilient, and positive you.

TABLE OF CONTENTS

"When negativity knocks, let positivity open the door and run the show!"

Shani T. Night

EMPOWERED BEGINNINGS

"I am my own greatest supporter. I talk to myself with kindness and encouragement. Every word I speak to myself is filled with positivity and motivation. I believe in my abilities, and I am capable of achieving great things. Today, I choose to focus on the positive and celebrate my successes. I am my own cheerleader, and I am proud of the person I am becoming."

Shani T. Night

WELCOME TO POSITIVE SELF TALK!

Definition: Positive self-talk refers to the practice of using optimistic and encouraging inner dialogue to influence your thoughts, emotions, and behaviors.

"Since we spend most of our lives in our own minds, let's decorate it with kindness, cultivate joy, and turn our thoughts into the coziest home for our hearts."

Shani T. Night

Positive self-talk is frequently underestimated and neglected, often not given due consideration in discussions about mental health. However, it has the potential to become your most powerful ally in nurturing your emotional well-being, molding your behavior, and influencing the overall state of your mental health.

The connection between self-talk and emotions is complex. The words we internally choose cast shadows, subtly influencing our feelings long before we consciously recognize their impact.

"Let the sweet tune of transformation resonate with a soulful sound like the symphony of your life."

Shani T. Night

In our thoughts, there exists a constant companion that rarely takes a break – our self-talk. It is the silent conversation we have with ourselves, the quiet stream of thoughts that flows through our minds effortlessly and subconsciously.

But have you ever stopped to think about the incredible impact your internal dialogue can have on your life?

I didn't until one day, I did, and it changed my life and helped me through some rough times.

Embrace the rhythm of change, for its tempo is uniquely yours. Dance with awareness, and ensure the melody of transformation is sweet.

Shani T. Night

Have you ever noticed that you talk to yourself more than anyone else?

It's like having a constant companion in your mind. So why not make that conversation a positive and uplifting one?

How we talk to ourselves has a powerful impact on how we feel. Instead of setting yourself up for failure, set yourself up for success.

Instead of being your own critic, be your biggest cheerleader. Embrace positive self-talk – those words of encouragement that uplift your spirits. The world has enough critics and far too many negative people.

Imagine being your own source of motivation, cheering yourself on through challenges. Your internal dialogue has the incredible ability to shape your mood, influence your beliefs, and impact your overall well-being. So, let's choose kindness over criticism and optimism over doubt.

"Walking in your truth is brave, and shining in
your purpose is divine. Anything else is
unimaginable."

Shani T. Night

Celebrate your successes, no matter how small. Remind yourself of your strengths and capabilities. When faced with challenges, be your own problem solver. Turn negative thoughts into positive affirmations. You have the power to create a positive atmosphere within yourself.

All of this is the goal of Positive Self-Talk.

"Embrace the rhythm of your own journey; every step is a note in the symphony of your life, creating a melody uniquely yours."

Shani T. Night

In this ongoing conversation with yourself, let every word reflect self-love and a belief that you are your biggest supporter. Once you do this, your positivity will lighten up your path. So talk to yourself with kindness, and watch how it transforms how you feel and navigate life. You are deserving of the uplifting words you speak to yourself!

Here's the truth: You would extend kind words to someone else who is talking negatively about themselves or needs positive encouragement. Why not extend this same grace to yourself? It makes sense.

Why is it so easy to do it for others but never for yourself?

Let's explore.

TRANSFORMING YOUR SILENT THOUGHTS

At the heart of our thoughts lies a dialogue that seldom meets the ears of others but resonates loudly within us – our self-talk. As we embark on an illuminating exploration of the complex thread or fabric of self-talk, an intricate phenomenon that serves as the foundation where our innermost thoughts, beliefs, and narratives form together to form the essence of our self-perception. As we peel back the layers of this internal conversation, we discover the subtle influences that shape our understanding of who we are, our place in the world, and our view of the world. Just as a mirror reflects our physical appearance, self-talk reflects our thoughts, exposing the stories we tell ourselves about our capabilities, worth, and potential. As we unravel these layers, we encounter the intricacies of our thought processes, discovering the beliefs that have silently etched themselves into the fabric of our consciousness. These beliefs, often formed through experiences, upbringing, and societal influences, act as the lenses through which we interpret ourselves and our surroundings.

Here, we are exploring self-talk and how this intimate conversation acts as a mirror reflecting our deepest insecurities, loftiest aspirations, and the untapped power residing within. Through relatable examples and thought-provoking insights, I invite you to witness the profound ways in which self-talk molds our perception of reality, guiding us toward a richer understanding of our innermost selves.

The narratives we construct within our minds become the guiding scripts that influence our reactions, decisions, and emotional responses. This exploration isn't merely an intellectual exercise but a journey into the very essence of what makes us who we are. By peeling back these layers, we gain insight into the shaping forces behind our perspectives, paving the way for self-awareness and the potential for intentional, positive transformation. In understanding these intricacies, we empower ourselves to consciously weave a tapestry that reflects a more authentic and empowered self.

"I am a source of love, acceptance, and support within myself. I recognize that people will be people, and I release the need to find these qualities in others. Before seeking love, acceptance, or support from outside, I give it generously to myself, nurturing a reservoir of strength and positivity within."
Shani T. Night

MAKING THE CONNECTION.

Self-talk plays a pivotal role in shaping our perception of reality and guiding us toward a richer understanding of our innermost selves through several interconnected mechanisms:

Filtering Information:
Our minds are bombarded with an overwhelming amount of information every day. Self-talk acts as a filter, selectively focusing on certain aspects while ignoring others. Positive self-talk allows us to filter in constructive and affirming elements, providing a more optimistic lens through which we perceive reality.

Interpretation of Events:
The way we interpret events is heavily influenced by our inner dialogue. Positive self-talk helps us interpret challenges as opportunities for growth rather than insurmountable obstacles. It reframes setbacks as temporary and encourages a more optimistic perspective, guiding us to learn from experiences rather than dwelling on perceived failures.

Emotional Influence:
Self-talk has a profound impact on our emotional responses. Positive self-talk fosters emotions such as resilience, confidence, and gratitude, influencing our overall emotional well-being. By cultivating a positive internal dialogue, we steer ourselves toward a more emotionally rich and fulfilling experience of reality.

Cognitive Bias Correction:
Negative self-talk aligns with cognitive distortions, such as overgeneralization, catastrophizing, and all-or-nothing thinking. Positive self-talk is a corrective lens, helping us identify and challenge these distortions. This correction leads to accurate and balanced perceptions of ourselves and the world around us.

Influence on Behavior:
Our self-talk guides our behavior by shaping our beliefs about our capabilities and worth. Positive self-talk instills confidence, encouraging proactive and constructive actions. It guides us toward behaviors that align with our values and aspirations, contributing to personal growth and a more fulfilling life.

Creation of Self-Fulfilling Prophecies:
The beliefs we reinforce through self-talk manifest as self-fulfilling prophecies. Positive self-talk instills confidence in our abilities, making us more likely to approach challenges with determination and resilience. This proactive mindset increases the likelihood of achieving success, reinforcing the positive beliefs that initiated the process.

Enhanced Self-Awareness:
Engaging in positive self-talk fosters a heightened sense of self-awareness. By regularly examining and reshaping our internal dialogue, we gain insights into our values, strengths, and areas for improvement. This increased self-awareness contributes to a richer understanding of our innermost selves and facilitates personal development.

In essence, our ongoing conversation with ourselves shapes the lens through which we perceive and interact with the world. Positive self-talk acts as a guiding force, steering us away from self-limiting beliefs and towards a reality that aligns with our authentic selves. Through this intentional shaping of our internal dialogue, we gain a deeper understanding of who we are, what we value, and how we can navigate the complexities of life with resilience and purpose.

"What you share can be the most powerful truth you tell."
- Shani T. Night

HOW SELF-TALK INFLUENCES YOUR EMOTIONS

Exploring the relationship between self-talk and emotions and its intricate connection and impact on how the words we choose to speak internally can cast shadows or illuminate our emotional landscape. Let's jump into examples that illustrate how self-talk can steer us toward feelings of empowerment, anxiety, confidence, or doubt.

In our inner world, self-talk emerges as the subtle yet potent whisperer of our emotions. I invite YOU to explore the delicate interplay between thoughts and feelings, unraveling the profound impact of self-talk on the emotional fabric of our lives. Like a composer, positive self-talk crafts uplifting melodies that resonate with joy, confidence, and resilience, elevating our emotional state.

Through engaging narratives and relatable examples, we illuminate the transformative power of choosing affirming thoughts, demonstrating how they become the harmonious notes that infuse our emotional experiences with positivity. Conversely, we delve into the darker corners where negative self-talk resides, dissecting its dissonant effects on emotions such as anxiety, fear, and self-doubt. This book is a journey into the heart of our emotional responses, unveiling how our internal dialogue shapes the symphony of feelings that color our daily experiences.

As we navigate this emotional landscape, I'll offer tools, definitions, guided reflections, exercises, and examples to help you change the narrative of how you talk to yourself on this journey of self-discovery so you can gain insight into the profound connection between self-talk and emotions, fostering a deeper understanding of your own emotions, empowering you to become intentional conductors of your emotional symphony, orchestrating emotional well-being through compassionate and purposeful crafting of your internal dialogue.

The words we choose to speak internally play a significant role in shaping our emotional landscape, casting shadows, or illuminating our inner world. The nature of our self-talk can steer us towards a spectrum of emotions, influencing our sense of empowerment, anxiety, confidence, or doubt. Here are examples illustrating how self-talk can have varying emotional impacts:

Empowerment:

Positive Affirmations: "I am capable and resilient. Challenges are opportunities for growth."

Encouragement: "I can overcome this obstacle by breaking it down into smaller, manageable steps."

Self-Validation: "I am worthy of success, and I believe in my abilities."

Anxiety:

Catastrophizing: "If I make a mistake, everything will fall apart, and it will be a disaster."

Overgeneralization: "I always mess things up. This will never work out for me."

Negative Prediction: "I know something bad is going to happen; I can feel it."

Confidence:

Positive Self-Talk: "I have prepared well for this presentation; I am knowledgeable and capable."

Self-Encouragement: "I've faced challenges before and succeeded. I can handle this."

Acknowledgment of Strengths: "I have unique talents and skills that contribute to my success."

Doubt:

Self-Criticism: "I should have done better. I'm not good enough."

Comparison: "Everyone else seems to have it figured out. I'm falling behind."

Fear of Failure: "If I try, I'll probably fail. It's safer not to take the risk."

The words we choose internally create a narrative that shapes our emotional responses. Positive and empowering self-talk fosters feelings of confidence, resilience, and empowerment. In contrast, negative or self-critical self-talk contributes to anxiety, self-doubt, and a lack of confidence. By becoming aware of these patterns, we intentionally shift our internal dialogue to cultivate a more positive emotional landscape and foster a healthier mindset.

The layers that make up the intriguing phenomenon of self-talk are intricate and interconnected, forming the very fabric of our understanding of ourselves and the world around us. These layers include thoughts, beliefs, and narratives that intertwine to shape our perceptions and influence our behaviors.

Thoughts:

At the core of self-talk are individual thoughts, the fleeting and often automatic stream of consciousness that runs through our minds. These thoughts can be positive or negative, constructive or destructive, and they serve as the building blocks of our inner dialogue.

Beliefs:

Beyond individual thoughts lie deep-seated beliefs. These are the convictions we hold about ourselves, others, and the world. Beliefs can be formed through personal experiences, cultural influences, and societal norms. They act as a filter through which we interpret information and events, influencing the tone and content of our self-talk.

Narratives:

Narratives are the stories we construct about ourselves and our lives. They bring coherence to our experiences and create a sense of continuity. Narratives incorporate our thoughts and beliefs, weaving them into a cohesive storyline that shapes our identity. Depending on the nature of our self-talk, these stories can be empowering or limiting, optimistic or pessimistic.

Core Values:

Embedded within the layers of self-talk are our core values — the principles and ideals that are fundamental to our sense of self. Our values guide our decision-making and contribute to our internal dialogue's moral and ethical dimensions.

Emotional Responses:

The layers of self-talk profoundly influence our emotional responses. Positive thoughts and beliefs contribute to a more optimistic emotional landscape, while negative or self-critical elements trigger feelings of anxiety, self-doubt, or sadness.

Worldview:

Our worldview, encompassing our perspectives on life, relationships, and broader societal issues, is shaped by the layers of self-talk. It influences how we interpret events, engage with others, and make sense of the world.

Self-Image:

Self-talk contributes significantly to forming our self-image — the mental picture we hold of ourselves. Positive self-talk fosters a healthy self-image, while negative self-talk erodes confidence and contributes to a distorted self-perception.

Decision-Making Framework:

The layers of self-talk serve as a decision-making framework, influencing our choices in various aspects of our lives. They guide our behaviors, responses to challenges, and the pursuit of goals.

Understanding these layers allows us to navigate the intricate landscape of self-talk more consciously. By examining and reshaping our thoughts, beliefs, and narratives, we gain insight into the foundational elements that shape our understanding of ourselves and the world, ultimately fostering personal growth and a more positive and authentic self.

To truly know and embrace love is to embark on a profound journey of self-discovery.

Shani T. Night

"Negativity breeds nothing but shadows. Choose the light, for it illuminates paths of possibility and growth." Shani T. Night

THINGS TO KNOW

HAPPY
IN
HAPPY
OUT

Positive self-talk is a powerful tool for improving mental well-being and achieving personal growth. Here are 20 essential things to know about positive self-talk aimed at integrating the 10 phases of adopting a constructive and optimistic inner dialogue.

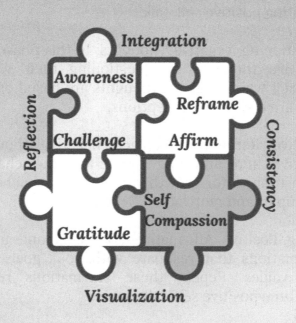

This journey is not strictly linear. Move at your own pace, and your pace will be defined by your experiences and personal growth. The key is to cultivate a mindful and intentional inner dialogue that promotes positivity and resilience.

10 PHASES OF ADOPTING A CONSTRUCTIVE AND OPTIMISTIC INNER DIALOGUE EXPLAINED

Positive self-talk involves adopting a constructive and optimistic inner dialogue to enhance mental well-being and overall positivity. The phases of positive self-talk can be conceptualized as follows:

1. Awareness:
   - Recognizing Negative Thoughts: The first phase involves becoming aware of negative or self-critical thoughts. Acknowledging when these thoughts arise is crucial for initiating positive self-talk.
2. Challenge:
   - Questioning Negative Thoughts: In this phase, challenge negative thoughts by questioning their validity. Ask yourself whether these thoughts are based on facts or if they are distorted perceptions.
3. Reframe:
   - Positive Reframing: Replace negative thoughts with positive and affirming ones. Reframe challenges as opportunities for growth, and consciously choose words that uplift and motivate.
4. Affirmation:
   - Using Positive Affirmations: Develop and use positive affirmations that resonate with your goals, strengths, and values. Repeat these affirmations regularly to reinforce positive self-talk.
5. Gratitude:
   - Focusing on Gratitude: Integrate gratitude into your self-talk. Reflect on positive aspects of your life, accomplishments, and the things you are thankful for, fostering a positive mindset.

6. Visualization:
   - Positive Visualization: Visualize successful outcomes and positive scenarios. This phase involves creating mental images of achieving your goals and experiencing positive events.
7. Self-Compassion:
   - Practicing Self-Compassion: Cultivate a kind and understanding attitude toward yourself. Treat yourself with the same compassion you would offer to a friend facing challenges.
8. Consistency:
   - Establishing Consistency: Positive self-talk is most effective when practiced consistently. Make it a habit to consciously choose positive thoughts and affirmations throughout the day.
9. Reflection:
   - Reflecting on Progress: Regularly assess your progress in adopting positive self-talk. Celebrate small victories and learn from setbacks, adjusting your self-talk patterns accordingly.
10. Integration:
   - Integrating Positive Habits: Positive self-talk becomes more ingrained when it is integrated into your daily routine. Make it a part of your lifestyle, allowing it to influence your overall mindset and well-being.

Again, these phases are not strictly linear, and you may move between them based on your experiences and personal growth.

The key is to cultivate a mindful and intentional inner dialogue that promotes positivity and resilience.

While self-talk is a continuous process, let's categorize it into three broad levels.

Automatic Self-Talk:

This level involves automatic and often unconscious thoughts that spontaneously arise in response to situations. These thoughts can be positive, negative, or neutral and are influenced by ingrained beliefs, past experiences, and emotional states.

Deliberate Self-Talk:

At this level, individuals consciously choose and direct their inner dialogue. Deliberate self-talk is intentional and purposeful, often used for goal-setting, problem-solving, and motivation. Positive affirmations and visualization techniques fall into this category.

Meta-Cognitive Self-Talk:

This level involves the awareness and analysis of one's own thoughts. Individuals engage in meta-cognitive self-talk when they reflect on their thinking patterns, question the validity of their thoughts, and consciously evaluate the impact of their inner dialogue on emotions and behaviors.

Each level of self-talk plays a role in shaping overall mental well-being. Automatic self-talk may reveal underlying beliefs and habits, deliberate self-talk empowers intentional thought choices, and meta-cognitive self-talk fosters self-awareness and emotional regulation. The interplay between these levels is dynamic, and individuals may move between them depending on the context and their emotional state. Developing a positive and constructive self-talk pattern often involves a combination of addressing automatic thoughts, incorporating deliberate affirmations, and fostering meta-cognitive awareness.

HERE ARE 20 IMPORTANT THINGS TO KNOW ABOUT POSITIVE SELF-TALK

Fill in the phases from the previous pages in the empty puzzle pieces at the top of each page in the following section.
Have Fun!

Awareness

Understanding the origins of negative self-talk is the first step toward challenging and changing these patterns.

Engaging in self-awareness, cognitive restructuring, and practicing positive self-talk counteracts the impact of negative thoughts and beliefs.

Awareness

Impact on Mood:
Engaging in positive self-talk elevates
your mood, reduces stress, and
increases feelings of happiness and
contentment.

Affirmation

Self-Affirmation:
Positive self-talk involves affirming your strengths, capabilities, and worth, which boosts self-esteem and confidence.

Challenge

**Cognitive Restructuring:
It's about challenging and replacing
negative or irrational thoughts with
more balanced and constructive ones.**

Affirmation

Internal Support:
Positive self-talk is your internal support system, providing comfort, reassurance, and motivation during challenging times.

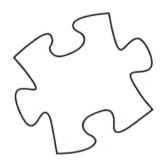

Reducing Self-Criticism:
By diminishing self-criticism and self-doubt, you cultivate a greater sense of self-compassion and understanding towards yourself.

Managing Challenges:
Positive self-talk equips you with the
tools to approach obstacles and
setbacks with a growth mindset, seeing
them as opportunities to learn and
improve.

Stress Reduction:
By focusing on positive aspects, you lower stress levels and prevent the harmful effects of chronic stress on your health.

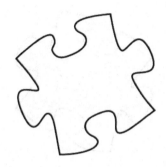

Boosting Resilience:
Developing a habit of positive self-talk enhances your resilience, enabling you to bounce back from adversity more effectively.

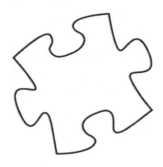

**Improved Performance:
Positive self-talk enhances
performance in various areas of life,
such as work, sports, and creative
endeavors.**

Integration

**Mind–Body Connection:
Positive self-talk positively influences
your physical health by promoting
relaxation and reducing the negative
impact of stress on the body.**

Consistency

Building Optimism:
Consistently practicing positive self-talk nurtures an optimistic outlook, leading to positive perceptions of the world around you.

Reframe

Language Choice:
The words you use in your self-talk
matter. Choosing constructive and
kind language shapes your perspective.

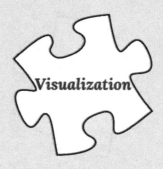

Visualization

Goal Achievement:
Positive self-talk helps maintain focus
on your goals, increasing your
determination and commitment to
achieving them.

Reality-Based Thinking:
Positive self-talk doesn't mean denying reality; it means interpreting situations realistically and emphasizing strengths and potential solutions.

Self-Compassion:
Embracing self-compassion enables you to extend the same kindness and understanding to yourself as you would a friend.

Breaking Patterns:
Positive self-talk assists in breaking
negative thought patterns, which leads
to decreased anxiety and depression
symptoms.

Gratitude

Cultivating Mindfulness: Engaging in positive self-talk encourages mindfulness, as it requires you to be present and aware of your thoughts.

Daily Practice:
Regular practice is key to making positive self-talk a habit, leading to long-lasting changes in thought patterns.

Integration

Personal Growth:
Embracing positive self-talk is a journey of personal growth and self-improvement, contributing to a more fulfilling and meaningful life.

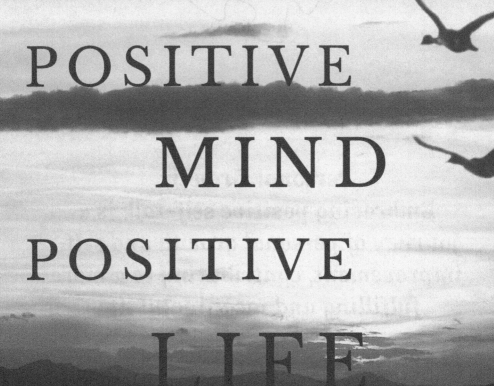

Integration

Remember that positive self-talk is a skill that takes time and practice to develop. By consistently nurturing a positive internal dialogue, you can transform your mindset and enhance your overall well-being.

EVICT

Negative

Self-Talk

FROM YOUR MIND

And

REPLACE IT WITH THE
RENT-FREE TENANTS OF
Positivity
&
Self-Love.

Shani T. Night

Before we jump into the practice exercises, there are a few more aspects I haven't addressed – specifically, the influence of self-talk on our emotions.

Self-Fulfilling Prophecy:

The way you talk to yourself influences your beliefs about your abilities. Positive self-talk reinforces a belief in your capabilities, increasing motivation and a greater likelihood of success. Conversely, negative self-talk creates a self-fulfilling prophecy of failure.

In embracing the concept of a Self-Fulfilling Prophecy, I've incorporated a ritual into my routine. I consciously radiate positive vibes before engaging in any activity, whether attending a meeting, meeting with a client, or facilitating an event. I affirm to myself that things will unfold exactly as I envision – I will excel, communicate effectively, and showcase all my capabilities. I reassure myself that I have the ability to handle any situation.

Consistently, when I genuinely believe and let these positive affirmations resonate within me, the outcomes have been outstanding. The events, meetings, or activities unfold smoothly, aligning with the positive expectations I set.

On the flip side, when I allow negative thoughts to creep in, the results tend to go awry. It reaffirms the power of mindset and how our beliefs shape our experiences. By maintaining a positive outlook, I not only set the stage for success but also cultivate an environment where my capabilities shine.

Impact on Coping Mechanisms:

During challenging situations, the nature of your self-talk influences your ability to cope. Positive affirmations and a constructive internal dialogue enhances resilience and problem-solving skills, while negative self-talk hinders effective coping strategies.

Perspective and Interpretation:

Self-talk shapes how you interpret events. Two people facing the same situation may have different emotional responses based on their internal dialogue. Positive self-talk helps reframe challenges as opportunities for growth.

Influence on Self-Image

Consistent positive self-talk contributes to a healthier self-image. It builds self-esteem and self-worth, while negative self-talk erodes confidence and contributes to feelings of inadequacy.

Mind-Body Connection:

The mind-body connection is powerful. Negative self-talk contributes to physical symptoms such as tension, headaches, or stomach discomfort, while positive self-talk has a soothing and calming effect.

I dedicated two weeks to a task I genuinely disliked, and the toll on my well-being was evident through severe migraines. Approaching each day with a profound sense of dislike had a detrimental impact on both my health and overall wellness. The experience was so challenging that I felt compelled to articulate my feelings through a quote, a therapeutic act to release and reset myself.

In that critical moment, I drew strength from my foundational knowledge and the reserves of confidence within me. I reminded myself of the work I had put in, the preparation I had undertaken, and my inherent capabilities. By tapping into these resources, I found the resilience needed to triumph over the difficulties presented during those two weeks.

"I have unleashed the extraordinary by embracing
the challenge in the now;
with positivity as my trusted ally,
leading the way to triumph."

Shani T. Night

"In the dance of life and the unimaginable, I took
the lead, letting positivity guide each bold step of
self-discovery."

Shani T. Night

"In the grand dance of life, I embraced the unimaginable, with each step guided by the melody of positivity. Through self-discovery, I paved my path, ensuring that no weeds dared to steal the spotlight beneath my feet."

Shani T. Night

Energy and Motivation:

Positive self-talk provides a boost of energy and motivation. When you encourage yourself with affirming statements, you are more likely to approach tasks with enthusiasm and a can-do attitude.

Being mindful of your self-talk and consciously choosing positive and supportive language contributes to better emotional well-being and resilience in the face of life's challenges. Developing a habit of cultivating a positive internal dialogue is a valuable skill for promoting mental health.

Imposter Syndrome:

Impostor syndrome is not necessarily negative self-talk in itself, but it often involves a pattern of negative thoughts and feelings about one's abilities and accomplishments. Impostor syndrome is a psychological phenomenon where individuals doubt their skills, talents, or achievements and have a persistent fear of being exposed as a fraud, despite evidence to the contrary.

The negative self-talk associated with impostor syndrome includes thoughts like "I don't deserve this success," "I'm not as competent as people think I am," or "I got lucky, and it's just a matter of time before others find out." These thoughts undermine self-confidence and contribute to feelings of inadequacy.

It's important to recognize and address impostor syndrome by practicing self-awareness, challenging negative thoughts, seeking support from others, and acknowledging one's accomplishments and capabilities. Positive self-talk and building self-confidence are crucial components of overcoming impostor syndrome.

"Be the kind of friend to yourself that you would be to others—speak words of encouragement, shower yourself with grace, and watch your self-confidence soar"

Shani T. Night

"As a happiness coach, let's talk about something many of us experience at some point—Imposter Syndrome. It's that nagging feeling that you're not as competent as others perceive you to be, despite evidence of your accomplishments. Remember, you are not alone in this, and it doesn't define your worth. Challenge those negative thoughts, acknowledge your achievements, and celebrate your uniqueness. Embrace the journey of growth, and know that you are deserving of success. You've got this!"

Shani T. Night

To know love is to know and love yourself!

Shani T. Night

LETS PRACTICE

Day 1: Start each day with this positive affirmation statement:

"I am my own greatest supporter. I talk to myself with kindness and encouragement. Every word I speak to myself is filled with positivity and motivation. I believe in my abilities, and I am capable of achieving great things. Today, I choose to focus on the positive and celebrate my successes. I am my own cheerleader, and I am proud of the person I am becoming."

Every day, acknowledge the unique set of gifts bestowed upon you. Cultivate the ability to harness your innate talents. Embarking on a journey of positivity and mindfulness can be a great initial step.

Additional Positive Affirmations:

I am worthy of success and happiness.

I am constantly evolving and improving.

I trust myself to overcome any challenges.

I attract positive opportunities into my life.

I am focused and determined to achieve my goals.

I embrace challenges as opportunities for growth.

I am resilient and can handle anything that comes my way.

I am confident in my ability to create a successful future.

Now Add:

Day 2: Positive Self-Talk Mirror Exercise: Look in the mirror and say positive affirmations aloud. (Do this each day.)

This is a significant confidence boost, and, more importantly, it enables you to perceive yourself in a new and positive light.

Day 3: Challenge Negative Thoughts: Identify negative thoughts and challenge them with positive ones.

Cultivating this habit is crucial. Whenever a negative thought arises, respond with a positive one. Recognizing patterns will allow you to anticipate the onset of negative self-talk and prepare you to counter it with a positive perspective.

Day 4: Daily Positive Reflection: Reflect on one positive thing that happened each day.

What a simple yet powerful way to enhance your overall mental and emotional well-being. It is a practice that can be easily incorporated into daily routines with long-lasting positive effects. It's a wonderful tool if you aim to feel good about yourself. You can begin by reflecting on one positive thing that occurred each day and observe the joy entering your life.

Day 5: Gratitude Journal: List things you're grateful for to shift focus to positive aspects.
or
Daily Gratitude List: Start by listing three things you are grateful for each day. These can be simple or significant aspects of your life.

Day 6: Positive Visualization: Imagine achieving your goals and envision a positive future.

Day 7: Positive Goals Setting: Set realistic and positive goals for yourself.

Day 8: Positive Quotes Board: Create a board with inspirational quotes to uplift your mood.

If you can't do a board, start following someone who posts daily positive quotes.

Day 9: Self-Reflection: Reflect on personal qualities or achievements that you are grateful for within yourself. This can contribute to building self-appreciation.

Day 10: Self-Compassion Break: Be kind to yourself during challenging moments. Instead of being overly critical or judgmental, offer yourself the same compassion you would give to a friend in need.

Day 11: Before leaving your bed, begin your day by expressing gratitude for being awake. Next, draw back the curtains or open your blinds to invite the uplifting joy of sunshine into your space.

This will start to brighten your daily mood.

Day 12: Mindful Breathing: Practice deep, mindful breathing to calm the mind.

Day 13: Gratitude Walk: Take a walk and focus on things you're grateful for in nature (or your immediate area).

Day 14: Mindfulness Meditation: Practice being present and observing thoughts without judgment.

Day 15: Mindful Eating: Practice being aware and positive during meals.

Day 16: Self-Compassion Break: Be kind to yourself during challenging moments.

Day 17: Take a step toward one of the goals you identified on Days 6 & 7.

Day 18: Celebrate Achievements: Acknowledge and celebrate even small accomplishments.
Now, celebrate the step you took on Day 17.

Day 19: Acts of Kindness: Perform small acts of kindness for yourself and others.

Day 20: Self-Compassion Break: Be kind to yourself during challenging moments.

Additional exercises:

- Surround Yourself with Positivity: Spend time with people who encourage and support you.

- Upbeat Playlist: Create a playlist with uplifting songs to boost your mood.

- Compliment Jar: Write down compliments you receive and read them when needed.

- Self-Love Letter: Write a letter to yourself expressing self-love and appreciation.

- Implement Self-Care

- Practice Self-love

Day 21:

Imagine your mind as a beautiful garden filled with the seeds of your thoughts and emotions. Positive self-talk is like the warm and nourishing sunlight that bathes this garden.

Just as plants thrive in the presence of sunlight, your mind flourishes when exposed to the rays of positivity.

Each positive affirmation is a drop of sunlight, encouraging the seeds of self-belief, confidence, and optimism to sprout and grow.

Just as plants need care and attention, your thoughts need the gentle touch of encouragement. Positive self-talk acts as the energy that fuels the vibrant colors of your mental landscape.

Conversely, negative self-talk can be likened to a shadow that obstructs the sunlight. It hinders the growth of your mental garden, casting gloom over the potential beauty within. By consciously choosing positive words and affirmations, you allow the sunlight to pierce through the shadows, fostering a lush and thriving inner world.

In this metaphorical garden of the mind, tend to your thoughts with the warmth of positivity. Watch as the flowers of self-confidence bloom and the fruits of resilience ripen. Embrace the sunlight of positive self-talk and witness the transformation of your mental landscape into a sanctuary of growth, joy, and well-being.

THIS IS POSITIVE SELF TALK!

"I am a beacon of positivity and resilience. In every conversation with myself, I choose words that inspire, uplift, and empower. My mind is a garden of affirmations where positivity blossoms in abundance. I embrace challenges as opportunities for growth, and I trust in my ability to overcome any obstacle.

Every day, I speak words of encouragement to myself, nurturing a mindset of optimism and self-belief. I celebrate my achievements, no matter how small, and acknowledge the progress I make on my journey. My self-talk is a reflection of the strength and courage that resides within me.

I radiate positivity, and it reflects in my thoughts, actions, and interactions with others. With each positive affirmation, I build a foundation of self-love and confidence. I am the architect of my own happiness, and my internal dialogue shapes a future filled with success, joy, and fulfillment."

Shani T. Night

Here are some positive affirmations you can use during your morning to energize and uplift yourself:

- "With each step, I am invigorated and filled with positive energy."
- "The morning air rejuvenates my mind, body, and spirit."
- "I am grateful for the opportunity to embrace this new day."
- "I release any tension and welcome a sense of calm."
- "My steps are a powerful affirmation of my commitment to my well-being."
- "I am surrounded by the beauty of nature, and it fills me with joy."
- "With every breath, I inhale positivity and exhale any negativity."
- "I am strong, healthy, and ready to embrace the opportunities of the day."
- "The rhythm of my steps aligns with the harmony of my mind and body."
- "I walk in gratitude, appreciating the simple pleasures of this morning stroll."
- "I walk in gratitude, appreciating the simple pleasures of this morning."
- "My walk is a sacred time for self-care and self-love."
- "As I move forward, I leave behind any worries and embrace a fresh start."
- "I am in sync with the natural flow of life, moving with purpose and joy."
- "Every step I take is a step toward a healthier and happier me."
- "The sunshine fuels my positivity, and I radiate that energy to the world."

Feel free to choose the affirmations that resonate most with you or create your own personalized statements.

Repeat them as you walk, allowing the positive words to guide your thoughts and set a positive tone for the rest of your day.

"I refuse to diminish my essence to fit into the confines of someone else's comfort. I am unapologetically myself, embracing the freedom to be genuine and true."

Shani T. Night

"I refuse to shrink my essence to fit into someone else's comfort zone. I am unabashedly, unapologetically me—take it or let your comfort be reshaped."

Shani T. Night

SELF-TALK REFLECTION

I MATTER
BECAUSE...
FILL IN YOUR
TRUTH.

Instructions: Take a moment to contemplate your strengths, distinctive qualities, and achievements that set you apart and contribute to your value. Approach this reflection with honesty and self-kindness. Acknowledging your worth will enhance your confidence and resilience. Embrace the uniqueness that makes you exceptional. Remember, you are truly amazing, and your significance is undeniable! Enjoy the process, and have fun celebrating yourself.
Note: This can be difficult at first, but once you start practicing, it will become easier. Fill in your truth.

Strengths:
- "I recognize my strength in staying persistent, even when faced with challenges."
- "One of my strengths is my ability to adapt to new situations and learn quickly."
- "I have a compassionate nature that allows me to connect with and support others."

Distinctive Qualities:
- "My creativity is a distinctive quality that adds a unique flair to everything I do."
- "I possess a strong sense of empathy, which helps me understand and connect with people on a deeper level."
- "My curiosity and openness to new ideas set me apart and contribute to my personal growth."

Achievements:
- "I am proud of the project I completed last month, showcasing my dedication and skills."
- "Receiving recognition for my contributions at work is a testament to my hard work and commitment."
- "Graduating from [school/program] demonstrates my ability to set and achieve significant goals."

Self-Kindness:
- "I appreciate the effort I put into self-improvement and acknowledge my progress."
- "It's okay to make mistakes; they are opportunities to learn and grow, and I forgive myself."
- "I treat myself with kindness, understanding that I am a work in progress."

Acknowledging Worth:
- "I am worthy of love, respect, and success in all areas of my life."
- "My contributions matter, and I bring value to the people and environments I engage with."
- "I deserve to prioritize my well-being and pursue my dreams with confidence."

Embracing Uniqueness:
- "I celebrate the unique perspectives and ideas I bring to the table."
- "My individuality is a strength that enriches the world around me."
- "I embrace my quirks and differences, recognizing that they make me who I am."

Enjoying the Process:
- "I find joy in the journey of self-discovery and personal growth."
- "Every step I take towards my goals is a reason to celebrate."
- "I am grateful for the opportunities that allow me to enjoy the process of becoming the best version of myself."

Feel free to use these examples as inspiration and adapt them to align with your own strengths, qualities, and achievements. The key is to express genuine appreciation for yourself and your unique contributions.

POSITIVE SELF-TALK

REFRAME
NEGATIVE
TO
POSITIVE...
FILL IN YOUR
TRUTH.

Instructions: Cultivate a habit of positive internal dialogue by consciously replacing self-critical thoughts with uplifting and supportive language.

Notice when negative thoughts arise and intentionally reframe them into positive statements. Be your own cheerleader and speak to yourself with kindness and encouragement. Focus on affirming your abilities, resilience, and potential for success. Consistent practice of positive self-talk can contribute to improved self-esteem and a more optimistic outlook on life.

Self-Confidence:

- Old thought: "I can't do this; it's too hard."
- Positive self-talk: "I may face challenges, but I have the skills and determination to overcome them. I can do this."

Handling Mistakes:

- Old thought: "I always mess things up."
- Positive self-talk: "Mistakes happen; they are opportunities to learn and grow. I'll use this as a chance to improve."

Facing Challenges:

- Old thought: "This is too overwhelming; I'll never get through it."
- Positive self-talk: "I'll take it one step at a time. I've overcome challenges before, and I have the resilience to tackle this too."

Body Image:

- Old thought: "I don't like the way I look."
- Positive self-talk: "I appreciate my body for all it does. I am unique, and I choose to focus on the things I love about myself."

Achieving Goals:

- Old thought: "I'll never reach my goals; it's too ambitious."
- Positive self-talk: "My goals are achievable with dedication and persistence. I believe in my ability to make progress."

Dealing with Stress:

- Old thought: "I can't handle this stress; it's too much."
- Positive self-talk: "I'll take a deep breath and tackle one thing at a time. I am capable of managing stress, and I'll get through this."

Social Situations:

- Old thought: "I'm not good in social settings; I'll embarrass myself."
- Positive self-talk: "I have interesting things to share, and people appreciate me for who I am. I can navigate social situations with confidence."

Remember, the key is to tailor these statements to your own experiences and challenges. It's about acknowledging negative thoughts and consciously replacing them with positive and constructive alternatives.

POSITIVE AFFIRMATION CRAFTING

EMPOWERING
STATEMENTS

FILL IN YOUR
TRUTH.

Craft positive and empowering statements to uplift and encourage yourself. Acknowledge your strengths, embrace your potential, and envision the positive impact you can make. Speak to yourself with kindness and optimism. Repeat these affirmations regularly to reinforce a positive mindset and nurture self-belief. Embrace the journey of self-empowerment with joy and enthusiasm. You are deserving of success, and your affirmations can shape a brighter and more fulfilling path ahead.

Self-Worth:
- "I am worthy of love and respect."
- "I embrace my uniqueness and recognize my value."
- "I am enough just as I am."

Courage and Resilience:
- "I have the strength to overcome any obstacle."
- "I am resilient, and I can handle whatever comes my way."
- "I am brave, and I trust in my ability to face challenges."

Success and Achievement:
- "I attract success into my life with my positive attitude."
- "I am capable of achieving my goals and fulfilling my dreams."
- "Every day, I am moving closer to my desired outcomes."

Positivity and Optimism:
- "I choose to focus on the positive in every situation."
- "I am surrounded by positivity, and my life is filled with joy."
- "I radiate positive energy and attract good things into my life."

Health and Well-being:
- "I prioritize my health and well-being, and I make choices that nourish my body and mind."
- "I am grateful for the strength and vitality in my body."
- "Every day, I am getting healthier and stronger."

- Abundance and Prosperity:
- "I am open to receiving abundance in all areas of my life."
- "I attract opportunities for success and prosperity."
- "I deserve to have abundance and prosperity flow freely into my life."

Gratitude:
- "I am grateful for the positive experiences and lessons in my life."
- "I appreciate the abundance of love and support around me."
- "Gratitude is the key to a happy and fulfilling life, and I am thankful for every moment."

Feel free to personalize these affirmations or create your own that resonate with your goals and aspirations. Repeat them regularly to reinforce a positive mindset and build self-confidence.

"How you respond to life and life situations is one of the most powerful truths you tell."
- Shani T. Night

EMPOWERED ENDINGS

As we arrive at the conclusion of this transformative journey, envision it not as a final chapter but as a launchpad for your empowered tomorrow. In these pages, you've woven a narrative of self-discovery, resilience, and positivity, crafting a blueprint for a future enriched by the echoes of your own affirming self-talk. As the curtain falls on this chapter, embrace the wisdom gained and let it be the compass guiding you toward a life fueled by the light of optimism. This conclusion marks not an end but a transition—an empowered beginning where the self-talk whispers you've nurtured become the driving force propelling you towards a brighter, more authentic, and purposeful tomorrow. Your story is a tapestry of strength, self-love, and growth, and with each positive affirmation, you're etching the vibrant lines of a future where your empowerment knows no bounds. Keep whispering words of kindness to yourself, for the conclusion is merely a prelude to the endless possibilities that await your continued journey of self-discovery and positive transformation.

EMBRACING YOUR JOURNEY OF POSITIVE SELF-TALK

Positive Self-Talk is a transformative journey, it's essential to reflect on the profound impact of positive self-talk in reshaping the landscape of our thoughts and emotions. Your commitment to exploring the intricacies of your inner dialogue is a testament to the resilience and courage within you. Remember that the power to cultivate a positive self-talk narrative lies within your daily choices, affirmations, and reflections.

In these pages, we've uncovered the layers of self-talk, from thoughts and beliefs to the narratives that shape our understanding of self and the world. The whispers of our internal dialogue serve as architects, molding our behaviors and influencing the decisions we make. By consciously crafting a blueprint of affirming and empowering self-talk, you've set the stage for a life guided by optimism, resilience, and self-compassion.

As you continue your journey, embrace the imperfections and setbacks as opportunities for growth. You hold the pen to your life's narrative, and with each positive affirmation, you rewrite the script, fostering a richer understanding of your innermost self. May the practice of positive self-talk be a constant companion, nurturing your confidence, enhancing your well-being, and leading you toward a future illuminated by the radiant glow of self-love and empowerment. Your story is a masterpiece in the making, and the echoes of your positive self-talk will resonate in every chapter, creating a life of purpose, joy, and authenticity. Keep whispering words of kindness to yourself, for you are the author of your own remarkable journey.

Remember, just as a mirror reflects our physical appearance, self-talk reflects our thoughts, exposing the stories we tell ourselves about our capabilities, worth, and potential. Let you self-talk reflect light, love, peace, joy, and above all truth.

"A lifetime can pass, feeling as though it's an eternity, without truly liking oneself. However, a profound transformation occurs when you discover your authentic self. Suddenly, appreciation blossoms, genuine and undeniable."

Shani J. Night

"One can spend a lifetime, or what seems like an eternity, pursuing to be someone else.
Yet, something magnificent happens when one realizes one's true self. You start living, but it's now authentic."

Shani T. Night

About the Author

My mission as a certified Happiness Life Wellness Coach is to help individuals live their happiest, healthiest, and most fulfilling lives. I believe that true happiness comes from within, and that by making positive changes in our thoughts, behaviors, and lifestyle, we can transform our lives and achieve lasting well-being.

I am committed to providing personalized coaching that is tailored to the unique needs and goals of each individual client. I believe that everyone has the potential to be happy and successful, and that my role is to provide guidance, support, and encouragement as my clients work to achieve their dreams.

I believe that wellness is a holistic concept that encompasses physical, emotional, and spiritual health, and that by addressing all aspects of wellness, we can achieve a more balanced and fulfilling life. Through my coaching, I aim to empower my clients to take control of their well-being and to make positive changes that will last a lifetime.

My goal is to create a safe, supportive, and non-judgmental space where my clients can explore their thoughts and feelings, overcome their challenges, and discover their true potential. I am passionate about helping others live their best lives, and I am dedicated to making a positive difference in the world, one client at a time.

From the Author

For me, happiness is finding contentment in my own skin, regardless of my location. It's embracing the radiance I emit and the positive energy I embody. True happiness lies in simply existing, free from the constraints of comparison or competition. It's about embracing both the favorable and challenging aspects of life and consistently embodying grace, compassion, and love. It involves acknowledging the inherent goodness in people, embracing them without judgment, and trusting a higher power to handle judgment while striving to be the best version of myself.

Moreover, it's recognizing that as a reflection of light, truth, compassion, grace, and love, I have the potential to positively impact those around me. I may serve as a beacon of inspiration, guiding others toward a better path and offering a source of light and support to those who need it. This awareness adds depth to my happiness, knowing that my journey is not only about personal fulfillment but also about contributing positively to the well-being of others.

*Knowing who you are is
it's own
appreciation.*

Books by Shani

- Intentionally Positive Path to Positive Change: A Guided Journal for Transformation Vol. I & II
- Intentionally Positive Planner: Positive Quotes, Affirmations, and Poems for daily life inspiration

Intentionally Positive Journals and Planners are sold on my website and on Amazon:
www.shanitnight.com/joyful

Take a little time to enjoy the view.

Made in United States
Orlando, FL
09 December 2024

55051002R00065